the VEGAN
Longevity Diet

Eat fat to live longer, slow ageing, reverse disease and faster-sustained weight loss

THE VEGAN LONGEVITY DIET

Eat fat to live longer, slow ageing, reverse disease and faster-sustained weight loss

ISBN 978-1-913005-35-1

DISCLAIMER

CONTENTS

DINNER RECIPES   43

SNACKS & DESSERTS   61

BONUS VEGAN DRINKS   79

INTRODUCTION

Of all the basic tenets of our lives, health is perhaps the most important. The vegan diet is one of the healthiest diets of all stemming from fresh, natural and wholesome foods.

Many of us still shun the vegan diet with the misguided idea that it's all about eating bland-tasting greens; which couldn't be further from the truth. We have compiled this cookbook as a beginners' guide to introduce you to the natural vegan lifestyle, complete with the most delicious recipes you'll ever eat without feeling meat deprived. We'll teach you that fat is not the enemy when it comes to shedding pounds and that in fact, a high-fat vegan diet can actually help and sustain weight loss.

Whether you have dabbled with veganism in the past, are a newbie adapting to a clean and healthy lifestyle or are looking to transition from a vegetarian lifestyle to a purely vegan lifestyle, this diet guide will hold your hand through the entire process.

This guide starts by introducing you to the origin of the vegan diet and how it has grown to be one of the most popular health movements of our time. It will also outline how to transition gently into the vegan diet with all the postive gains in addition to great health that you can expect.

You don't need to have any prior knowledge of the vegan diet or the vegan lifestyle in general. This guide will take you through all the important aspects and introduce you to some of the easiest and tastiest vegan recipes to help you follow a natural high-fat vegan lifestyle.

THE EVOLUTION OF VEGANISM

What's veganism?
Veganism is not a diet, but a lifestyle that completely avoids all animal products and any product derived from animals. This means eliminating foods such as dairy, honey and meat from your diet. The primary purpose of the vegan lifestyle is to restore balance in nature by protecting animals from cruelty and exploitation.

Veganism and vegetarianism are often used interchangeably but they don't mean the same thing. All vegans are vegetarians but not all vegetarians are vegans. There are different types of vegetarians – vegans, lacto vegetarians (they allow dairy consumption) and ovo vegetarians (allow the consumption of eggs).

In the beginning...

Veganism is not a modern philosophy. The Vegan Society was formed in 1944 but the vegan philosophy has been in existence for much longer with evidence of a vegan lifestyle dating back over 200 years ago. But, the real concept of a vegan way of life started taking shape in the 19th century with Dr. William Lambe and poet Percy Bysshe Shelley objecting to eggs and all dairy from an ethical standpoint.

In the modern day Donald Watson, founder of The Vegan Society, brought together common minded individuals comprised of non-dairy vegetarians to discuss the health benefits of their lifestyle and this evolved to what we now refer to as veganism.

Archeological evidence shows that some ancient civilizations made the conscious decision not to eat animals. Pythagoras, the Greek poet, followed what we now call the vegan diet in 500BC as he advocated showing kindness to all species. Around the same time, Buddha was also promoting a vegetarian lifestyle.

Veganism has actually grown out of necessity especially if we look at the eating habits of western society. By 2007 Americans were eating a whopping 220 pounds of meat and over 605 pounds of sugar. The escalating rate of chronic lifestyle illnesses, therefore, comes as no surprise. Today, animals are being restricted from their natural ways of life in the bid to increase their production of dairy, eggs and other products and also to increase their rate of reproduction for economical purposes. The circle of life has been interrupted by the greed of humankind.

The vegan diet is based on the sanctity of life. Animals should be left to freely thrive in their natural habitats without the fear of capture by human beings only to be forced to reproduce at unnatural rates.

The main premise of veganism is to use our control, intelligence and power to drive our planet in a way that does not exploit any animals and to co-exist peacefully and fairly with them. It is based on a plant based, whole food diet that is centered on purely natural and unrefined whole plants. The diet mainly focuses on fruits, veggies, legumes, tubers, nuts and whole grains. It excludes all meat – including fish, eggs, dairy foods, animal based oils, refined foods such as refined sugar, bleached flour and anything that can be linked back to animals during its production.

Devoted vegans hold true to their ethical convictions as they advocate for the environment and the increased energy and amazing health benefits they get from following the diet. Vegan foods continue to evolve from simple veggie dishes and salads to gourmet foods and are finally debunking the myth that veganism leaves you nutritionally deficient.

As veganism gains popularity, there is a revamped global movement to treat animals humanely and with respect and more and more people are willingly opting for a vegan lifestyle.

THE HEALTH BENEFITS OF THE HIGH FAT VEGAN DIET

- Clear, supple skin: Live plant based foods are very rich in antioxidants, vitamins and minerals which do a great job of eliminating toxic waste from your body and hydrating your skin; leaving you with beautiful and younger looking skin.

- Sleep like an angel: A plant based diet is friendly to all your bodily functions. The same cannot be said of animal based diets that usually overburden your digestive system meaning you don't get the required nutrition. The vegan diet ensures that your body functions optimally and when it comes to sleep time, you sleep like a baby as your bodily functions operate in the background.
- Increased energy: When your body is functioning optimally, thanks to a fresh and natural nutrient dense diet, you are sure to feel energetic with an increased mental focus.
- Increased metabolic rate: The vegan diet is exactly what man was meant to eat. As such, everything you eat that is vegan diet works to the benefit of your body including revving up your metabolism.
- Decreased lethargy: The vegan diet is the richest natural source of nutrients. This means that every part of your body is going to receive its required nutrition and so there will be no reason for you to feel deprived. The high fiber diet l keeps you full up to your next meal and you don't need to worry about fighting hunger pangs

WHAT TO EAT ON THE VEGAN DIET

- Fruits and veggies -   apples, bananas, mangoes, berries, grapes, broccoli, leafy greens, carrots, etc.
- Beans and legumes – lentils, lima beans, kidney beans, black beans, chickpeas, etc.
- Whole grains – quinoa, rice, whole wheat, barley, rice, oats, etc.
- Starch veggies and tubers – winter squash, potatoes, yams, celeriac, yucca, etc.
- Nuts and seeds – almonds, cashews, walnuts, flax seeds, pumpkin seeds, hemp seeds, etc.

This is definitely not an exhaustive list but the point to note is that the vegan diet is purely based on natural whole foods that have not been refined. A well-balanced diet will provide you with all the nutrition you need. Avoid all animal based foods and food products including cooking oil and also avoid refined food products that have very little nutrition. The goal here is to eat live plant based foods that are bursting with healthy nutrition.

HOW TO GET THE NUTRITION YOU NEED

The key to getting all the nutrients you need is eating a balanced vegan diet.

- Protein: We don't eat fish, meat, poultry or other animal based foods. These foods are high in protein which is important for our muscles and red blood cells. We need to find the best vegan substitutes that are also very high in protein such as soy products (edamame, tofu and fortified soy drinks); whole grains (buckwheat and quinoa); legumes (beans, lentils and dried peas); and nuts and seeds (almonds, cashews, walnuts, flax seeds, sesame seeds).
- Omega-3 fatty acids: These are essential for brain and heart health. You can get them from:
Natural oils (flaxseed oil, canola oil, soybean oil, walnut and olive oil); ground walnuts and flaxseed; and soybeans and tofu.
- Vitamins: Vitamins B12 and vitamin D help keep your blood cells and nerves healthy and also help your body absorb calcium. You can get these from:
Fortified vegan meat alternatives; fortified drinks made from almonds, rice and soy; and nutritional yeast.
- Minerals: Calcium, zinc, iron and other minerals are all very important for healthy and strong bones, a strong immunity and generally well-functioning body. You can get a healthy dose of minerals from: legumes, fresh fruits, sesame seeds, blackstrap molasses, fortified drinks, dried fruit such as prunes and whole grains.

WHY FAT IS GOOD FOR YOU?

Eating fats help keep you fuller longer and mean you won't be inclined to over eat which helps balance your overall weight and body health. Our brains need fat to function properly and consuming fat is also shown to improve cognitive functioning, ward off dementia, and decrease depression.

There's a reason the Mediterranean style of eating is so popular. High-fat diets (which include the right type of 'good' fats) can actually help prevent heart disease. Saturated fatty acids (found in nut butters and coconut oil) help white blood cells fight viruses and bacteria. The fats found in nuts have also been shown to lower cholesterol; reduce the risk of gallstones, heart disease, and diabetes; aid weight loss; and so much more.

We've made sure to include lots of high fat foods in our recipes so you'll get to benefit from both the goodness of a plant based diet as well as enjoying the benefits of good fats.

We've also included a bonus section of drinks to enjoy on your vegan diet. These aren't necessarily high in fat but will provide a great complementary addition to your diet.

Breakfast

LOW-CARB VEGAN PANCAKES

Vegan Breakfast

Ingredients

- 1 tbsp nut butter
- ½cup/120ml almond milk
- ¼ cup/30g coconut flour
- 1 tsp vanilla
- ½ tsp baking powder
- 2 tsp liquid stevia
- Pinch ground cinnamon
- Pinch salt

Method

1 In a large bowl, whisk all ingredients until well blended.

2 Put a greased nonstick frying on medium-low heat for a couple of minutes until hot.

3 Melt some of the butter. Pour about two tablespoons of batter into the pan and tilt the pan to spread evenly.

4 Cook for a couple of minutes each side until golden.

5 Transfer the pancake to a plate and repeat with the remaining batter.

CHEF'S NOTE
Top with plenty of chopped nuts and some vegan yoghurt for a high fat hit.

BERRY-INFUSED BREAKFAST QUINOA

Vegan
Breakfast

Ingredients

- ½ cup/90g cooked quinoa
- Handful frozen strawberries
- ¼ cup/40g cashews
- ¾ cup/175ml water

- ¼ cup /60ml coconut milk
- Toasted almonds and goji berries for topping

Method

1 User a blender to whizz together the cooked quinoa, strawberries, cashews and water until smooth.

2 Place the quinoa mixture in a serving bowl and stir in coconut milk.

3 Sprinkle with toasted almonds and goji berries to serve.

CHEF'S NOTE
Goji berries are also known as wolfberries which have long been used in traditional Asian cuisine.

BREAKFAST SLUSHIE SMOOTHIE

Vegan
Breakfast

Ingredients

- **1 ripe avocado**
- **¼ cantaloupe**

- **1 kiwi fruit**
- **Handful of ice**

Method

1 Peel the kiwi.

2 Add this, along with the avocado and cantaloupe melon, to a blender and blend until smooth.

3 Add a handful of ice, whizz again and serve immediately.

CHEF'S NOTE
Breakfast slushies offer a great vegan start to the day.

TASTY CHICKPEA VEGAN OMELETTE

Vegan Breakfast

Ingredients

- 2 tbsp coconut oil
- ½ cup/125ml coconut milk
- ½ cup/60g chickpea flour
- 2 tsp apple cider vinegar
- ¼ tsp onion powder
- ¼ tsp garlic powder
- ¼ tsp turmeric powder

- ¼ tsp baking soda
- ¼ tsp sea salt
- 2 garlic cloves, minced
- 1 red onion, chopped
- ½ head broccoli, chopped
- 2 large tomatoes, chopped

Method

1 In a bowl, whisk together the coconut milk, chickpea flour, apple cider vinegar, onion powder, garlic powder, turmeric powder, baking soda, and salt until well blended; leave to sit for 10 minutes.

2 Meanwhile melt the 1 tbsp coconut oil in a non-stick frying pan for a couple of minutes. Stir in onion, garlic and red onion and sauté for about 4 minutes or until lightly browned.

3 Add the broccoli and cook for about 5 minutes or until tender; transfer to a plate.

4 Add the rest of the coconut oil to the pan and pour in half of batter; add half of the broccoli mixture and tomatoes onto the batter and cook for about 2 minutes.

5 Gently fold one side of the pancake to cover the filling and cover the skillet; cook for about 5 minutes.

6 Transfer the pancake to a plate and keep warm. Repeat with the remaining batter and filling ingredients.

CHEF'S NOTE

Try serving with sliced avocado, lime wedges, and more red onion.

BERRY ACAI LUCUMA BREAKFAST

Vegan Breakfast

Ingredients

- ½ cup/75g blueberries
- ½ cup/75g blackberries
- ½ cup/75g raspberries
- ½ cup/75g goji berries
- 2 tbsp acai powder

- 1 tsp lucuma powder
- ½ avocado
- ½ frozen banana
- ½ cup/75g diced mango
- ½ cup/120ml almond milk

Method

1 Hold back a little of the fresh fruit for topping.

2 In a blender, blend all ingredients until very smooth.

3 Top up with ice cold water to make enough liquid to fill 3 tall classes.

4 Serve topped with the remaining fresh fruit.

CHEF'S NOTE

Lucuma is as a rich source of nutrients including beta-carotene, vitamin B3, iron, zinc, calcium & magnesium.

PROTEIN PACKED BREAKFAST CEREAL

Vegan Breakfast

Ingredients

- 6 medium dates, pitted
- 2 cups/240g chopped pecans
- 1 cup/120g pumpkin seeds
- 2 tsps cinnamon
- 1 tbsp vanilla extract

- ½ tsp sea salt
- ½ cup/75g dried blueberries
- 1 cup/80g unsweetened coconut flakes
- 1 cup/140g pomegranate seeds

Method

1 Preheat your oven to 325F/165C/Gas3

2 Add the dates and half the pecans to a food processor; pulse until finely ground.

3 Add the pumpkin seeds and the remaining pecans and continue pulsing until roughly chopped.

4 Transfer the mixture to a large bowl and add the cinnamon, vanilla and salt.

5 Spread on a baking sheet and bake for about 2 minutes or until browned.

6 Remove from the oven and leave it to cool slightly before stirring in the blueberries and coconut flakes.

CHEF'S NOTE

For even more vegan energy top with chopped banana and chia seeds.

BREAKFAST CITRUS SALAD WITH MINT

Vegan
Breakfast

Ingredients

- 1 navel orange, peeled and cut into rounds
- 1 grapefruit, peeled and cut into rounds
- 2 tsp liquid stevia
- 4 sprigs fresh mint
- 2 tbsp coconut yoghurt

Method

1 Arrange the fruit slices on individual plates and drizzle with liquid stevia.

2 Dollop over the yoghurt.

3 Top with mint sprigs and enjoy.

CHEF'S NOTE
Stevia is naturally very sweet but doesn't raise blood sugar levels like sugar and artificial sweeteners do.

SERVES 4

DETOX BREAKFAST SMOOTHIE BOWL

Vegan Breakfast

Ingredients

- 2 cups/300g frozen blueberries
- 1 tsp spirulina powder
- 1 scoop protein powder
- Juice of ½ lemon
- 1 cup/250ml organic coconut milk

- 1 tbsp shredded coconut
- 8 sliced strawberries
- 2 tbsp milled flax seed
- 1 tbsp chia seed
- 1 tbsp pumpkin seeds

Method

1 Combine the frozen blueberries, spirulina, protein powder, lemon juice and coconut milk in a blender.

2 Blend until very smooth and serve in bowls or tall glasses topped with the remaining seeds and berries.

CHEF'S NOTE

Spirulina contains significant amounts of calcium, niacin, potassium, magnesium, B vitamins and iron.

HEALTHY AVOCADO BREAKFAST SHAKE

SERVES 2

Vegan Breakfast

Ingredients

- 1 tsp matcha green tea powder
- ½ medium avocado
- ½ scoop vanilla protein powder
- 2 tsp liquid stevia
- 2 tbsp flax seeds
- 2 cups/500ml unsweetened almond milk

Method

1 Peel and de-stone the avocado.

2 Combine all the ingredients in a blender.

3 Blend on high until very smooth.

4 Serve in tall glasses and enjoy!

CHEF'S NOTE

Matcha contains unique antioxidants known as catechins which aren't found in most other foods. In particular, the catechin EGCg (epigallocatechin gallate) provides potent cancer-fighting properties.

POWER BREAKFAST CHIA PUDDING & BLUEBERRIES

Vegan Breakfast

Ingredients

- ½ cup/35g chia seeds
- 1½ cups/270ml almond milk
- 1 tsp ground cinnamon
- 1 tsp vanilla essence
- 1 tsp liquid stevia
- 2 handfuls blueberries

Method

1 In a bowl, stir together all the ingredients (except the berries) until well combined.

2 Let sit overnight to soak well.

3 When ready to serve, divide into serving bowls.

4 Garnish each serving with berries.

CHEF'S NOTE

Chia seeds are an excellent source of omega-3 fatty acids, rich in antioxidants, fibre, iron, and calcium.

SERVES 1 — COCONUT CINNAMON YOGHURT

Vegan Breakfast

Ingredients

- ¾ cup/175ml coconut yoghurt
- ½ tsp ground cinnamon
- 1 tbsp pumpkin seeds
- 1 tsp stevia

Method

1 Add yoghurt to a serving bowl.

2 Stir in the ground cinnamon and stevia until well combined.

3 Top with pumpkin seeds.

CHEF'S NOTE
Toast the pumpkin seeds in a dry pan before serving if you wish.

SPICY GLUTEN-FREE PANCAKES

Ingredients

- 4 tbsp coconut oil
- 1 cup/250ml coconut milk
- ½ cup/60g tapioca flour
- ½ cup/60g almond flour
- 1 tsp salt
- ½ tsp chilli powder

- ¼ tsp turmeric powder
- ¼ tsp black pepper
- ½ inch ginger, grated
- 1 pepper, de-seeded and finely chopped
- 1 handful fresh coriander, chopped
- ½ red onion, chopped

Method

1 In a bowl, combine together the coconut milk, tapioca flour, almond flour and spices until well blended.

2 Stir in ginger, pepper, coriander, and red onion.

3 Melt ¼ of the coconut oil in a nonstick frying pan over medium low heat.

4 Add ¼ of the batter and tilt the pan to spread it evenly spread out on the pan.

5 Cook for about 4 minutes per side or until golden brown.

6 Transfer to a plate and keep warm.

7 Repeat with the remaining batter and oil.

CHEF'S NOTE

Try adding some edamame for extra good fats.

HEALTHY BREAKFAST PARFAIT

SERVES 4

Vegan Breakfast

Ingredients

For the Base:
- ½ cup/70g pumpkin seeds
- ¼ cup/35g flax seeds
- ¼ cup /35g chia seeds
- 1 cup raw/120g walnuts
- 1 cup raw/120g almonds

For The Cashew Cream:
- 1 cup/120g raw cashews, soaked for 2 hrs
- ¼ tsp cinnamon
- ½ tsp vanilla
- 1 tsp liquid stevia
- ⅓ cup/80ml water
- ¼ tsp salt

Method

1 To make the base combine all nuts and seeds in a food processor and process into coarse meal.

2 To make the cashew cream combine all the ingredients in a blender and blend until very smooth and creamy.

3 In a serving glass, layer berries, then seeds and nut meal, and finally top with the cashew cream.

4 Sprinkle with more seeds and nut meal and garnish with berries.

5 Serve.

CHEF'S NOTE

Walnuts contain good fats, such as monounsaturated and polyunsaturated fats and they are also a good source of the essential fatty acid omega-3.

NUTTY FRUIT BREAKFAST

Vegan
Breakfast

Ingredients

- 1 cup/250ml coconut
-

- 2 oranges
- 1 cup/150g cranberries
- 1 cup/120g walnuts

Method

1 Peel the oranges and divide into segments removing as much of the white pith as you can.

2 Slice each segment into three.

3 Chop the walnuts.

4 In two serving glasses, alternate the layers of coconut yoghurt, orange slices, and cranberries.

5 Top with chopped walnuts to serve.

CHEF'S NOTE

The probiotics in coconut yoghurt help balance your gut health.

CREAMY STRAWBERRY BANANA PROTEIN SHAKE

Vegan
Breakfast

Ingredients

- 2 tsp ground chia seeds
- ½ tsp vanilla extract
- ½ scoop vanilla protein powder
- ½ cup orange juice

- 1 banana, frozen
- ⅔ cup/160ml almond milk
- ½ cup/75g frozen strawberries

Method

1 Combine all ingredients in a blender.

2 Blend until very smooth and enjoy.

CHEF'S NOTE
Almond milk is naturally rich in several vitamins and minerals, especially vitamin E.

Lunch

VEGAN DETOX SALAD

SERVES 2

Vegan
Lunch

Ingredients

- 2 cups/300g red cabbage, chopped
- 2 cups/300g kale, chopped
- 1 red onion
- 1 head cauliflower, roughly chopped
- 2 cups/300g baby carrots
- 2 tbsp fresh coriander, chopped
- ½ cup/70g sunflower seeds

- ½ cup/70g raisins
- ½ cup/70g raw hemp hearts

Citrus Dressing:
- 2 tbsp fresh lime juice
- 2 tbsp fresh lemon juice
- 1/3 cup/80ml apple cider vinegar

- ½ avocado
- 2 cloves garlic
- 2 tsp fresh coriander
- 2 tsp minced ginger
- 2 tsp maple syrup
- 2 tsp sea salt
- Pinch pepper

Method

1 Combine the cabbage, kale, cauliflower, onion, carrots and coriander in a food processor to shred.

2 Transfer the shredded vegetables to a large bowl and fold in sunflower seeds, hemp hearts and raisins.

3 Combine all dressing ingredients in a blender and blend until very smooth.

4 Serve the salad in salad bowls drizzled with the citrus dressing.

CHEF'S NOTE
Hemp seeds are exceptionally rich in two essential fatty acids; linoleic acid and alpha-linolenic acid.

SATISFYING GRILLED MUSHROOMS

Vegan Lunch

Ingredients

- 2 cups/300g shiitake mushrooms
- 1 tbsp balsamic vinegar
- ¼ cup/60ml extra virgin olive oil
- 2 garlic cloves, minced
- Handful of chopped parsley
- 1 tsp salt

Method

1 Rinse the mushrooms and pat dry; put in a foil and drizzle with the balsamic vinegar and extra virgin olive oil.

2 Sprinkle the mushroom with the garlic, parsley, and salt.

3 Grill for about 10 minutes or until tender and cooked through.

4 Serve warm.

CHEF'S NOTE

Shiitake mushrooms are prized for their rich, savoury taste and diverse health benefits. Try serving with some grated vegan cheese.

MIXED GREEN SALAD WITH SAGE & SQUASH

SERVES 4

Vegan
Lunch

Ingredients

- 2 Romaine lettuce
- 2 apples, cut into matchsticks
- 2 butternut squash, peeled, roasted & cubed
- Pinch of sea salt
- Pinch of pepper
- 3 tbsp olive oil
- ¼ cup/60ml fresh lemon juice
- 2 tbsp chopped sunflower seeds

Method

1 Pull apart the lettuce leaves, place in salad bowls and top with the apple matchsticks and roasted squash.

2 Sprinkle with salt and pepper and drizzle with olive oil and fresh lemon juice.

3 Toss and serve right away sprinkled with sunflower seeds.

CHEF'S NOTE
Butternut squash is a great source of fibre, as well as vitamins A, C, E and B along with calcium, magnesium, and zinc.

SUPER RAW POWER SALAD

Vegan
Lunch

Ingredients

For the Dressing:
- ¼ cup/60ml white apple cider vinegar
- ¾ cup/180ml extra virgin olive oil
- 1 tsp liquid stevia
- Pinch garlic powder
- Pinch sea salt

For the Salad:
- 2 apples, finely chopped
- Handful of beansprouts
- ½ cup/75g edamame
- ¾ cup/100g dried berries
- 1½ cups/225g chopped purple cabbage
- 4 cups/600g finely chopped kale
- ½ cup/70g raw sunflower seeds
- Pinch of sea salt
- Pinch of pepper

Method

1 In a sealable jar, mix all dressing ingredients and shake until well blended.

2 In a large bowl, mix all salad ingredients; pour over the dressing and toss to coat well.

3 Divide into bowls.

4 Season with salt and pepper and serve.

CHEF'S NOTE
Despite their small size, sunflower seeds are a dense source of vitamins, minerals and essential oils.

SYSTEM RESET SOUP

SERVES 4

Vegan
Lunch

Ingredients

- 2 tbsp coconut oil
- 2 garlic cloves, minced
- ½ red onion, chopped
- 2 carrots, diced
- 2 celery stalks, diced

- 1 cup/200g tinned chickpeas
- 1 cup/150g chopped broccoli
- 4 cups/1lt vegetable stock
- Sea salt

Method

1 Place a large saucepan over a medium heat and melt the coconut oil.

2 Sauté the celery, garlic, carrots, and onion for a few minutes or until tender.

3 Stir in chickpeas and broccoli and cook for 2 minutes more.

4 Stir in the stock and bring to a boil.

5 Lower the heat and simmer for 10 minutes or until the veggies are tender.

6 Remove the pot from heat and season with salt. Enjoy!

CHEF'S NOTE
Use a blender if you prefer your soup to be smooth.

AVOCADO, FENNEL & TOMATO SALAD

Vegan Lunch

Ingredients

- 1 large avocado, sliced
- 1 red onion, thinly sliced
- 1 large fennel bulb, chopped
- 4 medium tomatoes, chopped
- 1 tbsp avocado oil
- 3 tbsp extra virgin olive oil

- 2 tbsp fresh lime juice
- 2 tbsp chopped fresh coriander
- Pinch of chilli powder
- Pinch of smoked paprika
- Pinch of sea salt

Method

1 In a bowl combine together the avocado, red onion, fennel, and tomatoes to assemble the salad.

2 In a small separate bowl, whisk together the avocado oil, extra virgin olive oil, lime juice, coriander, chilli powder paprika and salt.

3 Pour over the salad and toss to combine well.

CHEF'S NOTE

Also known as the 'butter fruit', the avocado is the only fruit that provides a substantial amount of healthy monounsaturated fatty acids.

SUPERFOOD DETOX & CLEANSE SALAD

Vegan Lunch

Ingredients

- 1 cup/150g fresh blueberries
- 1 cup/150g carrots
- 5 cups/150g baby spinach
- 12 raw almonds, sliced

- 2 dates, pitted and diced
- 1 tbsp fresh lemon juice
- 2 tbsp extra-virgin olive oil

Method

1 Use a grater to shred the carrots.

2 Mix all the ingredients, except the lemon juice and olive oil, in a large bowl.

3 Whisk together olive oil and lemon juice and pour over the salad.

4 Toss to combine well and serve.

CHEF'S NOTE

The health benefits of almonds include lower blood sugar levels, reduced blood pressure and lower cholesterol levels.

SERVES 4

RED ONION CUCUMBER SALAD

Vegan
Lunch

Ingredients

- 2 large cucumbers, sliced
- 1 red onion
- 1 large tomato, diced
- 2 tbsp fresh lemon juice
- 125g/4oz vegan Greek style cheese
- Pinch of sea salt
- Pinch of pepper

Method

1 In a salad bowl, mix together the cucumbers, chopped red onion and chopped tomatoes.

2 Drizzle with lemon juice and sprinkle with pepper and salt.

3 Toss to combine well.

CHEF'S NOTE

'Violife' is a good vegan cheese, but use whichever you prefer.

CREAM OF BUTTERNUT SQUASH & GINGER SOUP

Vegan
Lunch

Ingredients

- 2 butternut squash, peeled & diced
- 1 tsp olive oil
- 1 tsp minced ginger
- 1 large onion, roughly chopped
- 4 cups/1lt vegetable stock
- 1 sprig of sage

- ¼ tsp, nutmeg
- ¼ tsp sea salt
- ¼ tsp black pepper
- ½ cup/70g toasted pumpkin seeds, for garnish

Method

1 Gently sauté the onion and ginger in the olive oil for a few minutes in a large saucepan.

2 Add all the other ingredients, except the pumpkin seeds, and bring to the boil. Lower the heat and leave to simmer for 20 minutes or until all the ingredients are tender.

3 Remove from the heat and blend until smooth.

4 Sprinkle with pumpkin seeds and serve.

CHEF'S NOTE
Pumpkin seeds are rich in antioxidants, iron, zinc, magnesium and many other nutrients.

LENTIL RED CURRY & COCONUT MILK SOUP

Vegan Lunch

Ingredients

- 3 cloves of garlic, minced
- 1 tbsp coconut oil
- 1 large onion, diced
- Pinch of red pepper flakes
- Pinch ginger powder
- 2 tbsp vegan red curry paste

- 1 cup/200g lentils
- 2 cups/300g chopped tomatoes
- 3 cups/750ml vegetable broth
- 1 cup/30g chopped spinach
- 1 cups/250ml coconut milk

Method

1 Gently sauté the onion and garlic in the coconut oil for a few minutes in a large saucepan.

2 Add all the other ingredients to the pan, except the coconut milk, and bring to the boil.

3 Lower the heat and leave to simmer for 20-30 minutes or until all the ingredients are tender.

4 Remove from the heat and blend until smooth.

CHEF'S NOTE

Lentils are an excellent source of molybdenum and folate.

BERRY SALAD WITH CITRUS STRAWBERRY DRESSING

Vegan
Lunch

Ingredients

For the Salad:
- ¼ cup/35g blueberries
- ½ cup/75g chopped strawberries
- 1 cup/30g mixed greens
- 2 cups/60g baby spinach
- 4 spring onions
- ½ avocado, sliced
- 1 carrot, shredded

For the Dressing
- 1 tbsp extra-virgin olive oil
- 2 tbsp apple cider vinegar
- ¼ cup/60ml fresh orange juice
- 5 strawberries

Method

1 In a blender, blend together all dressing ingredients until smooth.

2 Combine all the salad ingredients in a large bowl.

3 Drizzle with dressing and toss to coat well before serving.

CHEF'S NOTE

Use whichever type of greens are in season.

COCONUT LENTIL SOUP WITH GINGER & LEMONGRASS

SERVES 6

Vegan
Lunch

Ingredients

- 1 tbsp nut butter
- 6 cups/1½ lt vegetable broth
- 1 red onion, diced
- 2 cups/400g red lentils
- 2 kaffir lime leaves
- 1 tbsp chopped fresh garlic
- 1 tbsp grated fresh ginger

- 1 tbsp lemongrass paste
- 1 cup/250ml coconut milk
- 1 butternut squash, peeled & diced
- 1 tbsp curry powder
- Pinch of sea salt
- 4 spring onions, sliced
- 1 tbsp fresh coriander, chopped

Method

1 Gently sauté the red onion in the nut butter over a medium heat.

2 Combine the vegetable broth, red onion and lentils in a large saucepan, along with the onions and bring to the boil.

3 Cover and simmer for about 25 minutes or until lentils are tender.

4 Stir in kaffir lime leaves, garlic, ginger, lemongrass paste, coconut milk, diced squash, curry powder, and salt and simmer for a further 10 minutes.

5 Place in a blender to process until smooth.

6 Garnish with green onions and coriander to serve.

CHEF'S NOTE
This is great served over steamed vegetables

EDAMAME CHICKPEA POWER SALAD

SERVES 6

Vegan Lunch

Ingredients

For the Dressing :
- 1 large avocado
- 1 inch ginger root
- 1 shallot
- 3 tbsp fresh lime juice
- 1 tbsp apple cider vinegar
- 2 tsp pure maple syrup

- 1 tbsp extra-virgin olive oil
- 3 tbsp chopped fresh basil

For The Salad
- 1 cup/200g tinned chickpeas
- 2 tsp extra-virgin olive oil
- Pinch of ground ginger
- Pinch of ground cayenne pepper

- Pinch of ground cumin
- Pinch of sea salt
- ½ cup/60g cashews
- 1½ cup/225g chopped apples
- 1 cup shelled cooked edamame
- Salt and pepper
- 1 tbsp fresh basil, chopped

Method

1 Combine all the dressing ingredients in a blender and process until smooth.

2 Heat a saucepan over high heat and toast the chickpeas for a few minutes or until browned.

3 Remove from the heat, drizzle with olive oil and sprinkle with ginger, cayenne pepper, cumin and salt.

4 Stir until well coated and then combine in the cashews.

5 Return to the heat and cook over a medium heat for a few minutes or until the cashews are lightly browned.

6 In a medium bowl, combine the chickpea mixture with apples and edamame and season with salt and pepper.

7 Add the dressing and toss to coat well.

8 Garnish with basil and serve.

CHEF'S NOTE
Chickpeas are a good source of protein, carbs, fibre & fat.

MIXED VEGGIE SALAD WITH FRESH PEAS

Vegan
Lunch

Ingredients

- 1 large bunch curly kale, chopped into bite-sized pieces
- 1 cup/150g fresh peas, chopped
- 1 red pepper, deseeded & chopped
- 1 carrot, peeled and cut into ribbons using a julienne peeler
- 1 shallot, finely sliced

- A handful each of basil and coriander, chopped
- 1 avocado, cubed
- Fine sea salt, to taste

For the vinaigrette:
- ¼ cup/60ml extra virgin olive oil
- 1 tbsp finely grated fresh ginger

- 2 tsp freshly squeezed lime juice
- 3 cloves garlic minced
- 2 tbsp rice vinegar

Method

1 Place the kale in a large bowl and sprinkle with the sea salt. Gently massage the kale using your hands until soft and fragrant.

2 Toss in the remaining salad ingredients until well combined.

3 Whisk the vinaigrette ingredients then drizzle over the salad and toss well to combine.

CHEF'S NOTE

Once an obscure veg; Kale has become incredibly popular over the last 10 years and is now readily available almost everywhere.

Dinner

FREEKEH WITH ROASTED CAULIFLOWER

Vegan
Dinner

Ingredients

- **For the freekeh:**
- 1¼ cups/280g cracked freekeh
- ¼ cup/35g sliced almonds
- 2 cloves garlic, minced
- 1 tbsp olive oil
- ¼ tsp coriander
- ½ tsp salt

- ¼ tsp cumin
- 3 cups/750ml vegetable stock
- **For the cauliflower:**
- 1 large cauliflower, cut into florets
- 3 tbsp olive oil
- Black pepper and salt to taste

- **Tahini sauce:**
- 2 tbsp tahini
- 2 cloves garlic, minced
- 3 tbsp lime juice
- 1/3 cup/80ml water
- Pinch of red pepper flakes
- Pepper & salt to taste

Method

1 Preheat your oven to 425F/200C/Gas 7.

2 Arrange the cauliflower in a baking sheet and toss with salt, pepper and olive oil. Roast for half an hour or until golden brown, turning halfway through cooking.

3 Meanwhile, add a tbsp of olive oil to a non stick frying pan and place over a medium heat.

4 Add the almonds and sauté for 3 minutes or until gently browned.

5 Add the freekeh and cook for 2 minutes before adding the remaining dry ingredients and cook for a minute or two.

6 Pour in the stock and bring to a boil. Lower the heat and simmer for 25-30 minutes or until tender (add a little more stock if needed).

7 Drain any excess liquid and remove from heat, season and use a fork to fluff.

8 Whisk the dressing ingredients until smooth.

9 Serve the freekeh and roasted cauliflower and top with the tahini sauce.

CHEF'S NOTE
Garnish with sesame seeds, chopped coriander & raisins.

GREENED PAPRIKA MUSHROOMS

Vegan Dinner

Ingredients

- 1 cup/30g baby spinach, coarsely chopped
- 2 cups/300g green peas
- 2 garlic cloves, crushed
- 1-2 tsp paprika

- ½ large red onion
- 2 cups/200g mushrooms
- 3 tbsp extra virgin olive oil
- Pinch sea salt

Method

1 Place the oil in a large frying pan over a medium heat and sauté the onions and garlic for a few minutes.

2 When the onions are golden brown, add the mushrooms & paprika and cook until softened.

3 Add the spinach, peas & sea salt, turn down the heat and cook for a couple of minutes until everything is piping hot.

4 Season & serve

CHEF'S NOTE

Adjust the quantity of paprika to suit your own taste and try stirring through a little vegan yoghurt for more good fats.

MUNG BEAN & SPINACH STEW

SERVES 3

Vegan
Dinner

Ingredients

- 2 tsp sesame oil
- ½ cup/75g diced carrots
- ½ cup/75g chopped celery
- 1 cup /150g chopped leeks or onions
- 2 garlic cloves, minced
- 1 tsp minced ginger

- 1 tbsp date paste
- 2 tbsp nut paste (walnuts and pumpkin seeds)
- 1-2 tsp lemon/lime juice
- 1 tsp allspice
- ¼ tsp cardamom powder
- 2 tsp cumin powder

- ½ tsp black pepper
- Pinch salt & chilli flakes
- 4 cups/1lt veg stock
- ½ cup/15g spinach
- 1 cup/200g cooked yellow mung beans

Method

1 Heat oil in a large saucepan over medium high heat.

2 Sauté all the ingredients in the pan, except the spinach, stock, spinach and mung beans.

3 Cook for about 10 minutes and then add the stock, spinach and mung beans; simmer for a few minutes until piping hot then remove from heat.

CHEF'S NOTE
Serve with cubed avocado & chopped fresh tomatoes.

VEGGIES IN COCONUT CURRY SAUCE

Vegan Dinner

Ingredients

- 150g/5oz firm tofu, cubed
- 3 cups/450g carrots, sliced
- 2 heads of broccoli, cut into florets
- 1 cup/150g fresh peas
- 3 garlic cloves, thinly sliced
- 2 onions, thinly sliced

- 1 cup/250ml vegetable stock
- 1 cup/250ml coconut milk
- 2 tbsp coconut oil
- 1 tbsp fresh lemon juice
- 2 tsp curry powder
- Freshly ground black pepper

Method

1 Heat two tbsp of oil in a non stick frying pan. Sauté the garlic, onion, tofu and curry powder for 5 minutes.

2 Add the carrots, broccoli, peas, and salt and continue to cook for a further few minutes.

3 Stir in the stock, coconut milk, and lemon juice; cover and cook for about 12 minutes or until everything is tender and piping hot.

CHEF'S NOTE

The calories and healthy fats in coconut milk combine together to provide top-notch vegan fuel.

SAUTÉED GREEN BEANS & COURGETTES

Vegan
Dinner

Ingredients

- 1 tbsp extra virgin olive oil
- 60g/2oz green beans, chopped
- 1 courgette, thinly sliced
- A pinch of salt

- 2 tbsp lemon juice
- 2 spring onions, sliced
- Handful of black olives, sliced

Method

1 Add half of the oil to a frying pan set over medium heat.

2 Stir in green beans, courgettes & salt and sauté, stirring, for about 10 minutes or until the veggies are tender.

3 Remove the pan from heat and stir in lemon juice, olives and spring onions.

4 Serve immediately.

CHEF'S NOTE
Try serving with grated vegan cheese sprinkled over the top.

GINGER AND LEAFY GREENS STIR-FRY

Vegan Dinner

Ingredients

- 1 tbsp coconut oil
- 150g/5oz firm tofu, cubed
- 1 onion, finely sliced
- 2 garlic cloves, peeled and chopped
- 1 piece of ginger, chopped

- ½ squash, seeded, diced
- ¼ Savoy cabbage
- 2 handfuls of chopped leafy greens (spinach, kale, or chard)
- 1 tbsp soy sauce
- Fresh juice of ½ a lemon

- 1 red or green chilli, finely chopped
- A pinch of sea salt
- 1 pinch of freshly ground pepper
- A little water

Method

1 In a large frying pan set over medium heat, heat the coconut oil and sauté the onion and tofu for a few minutes.

2 Stir in garlic, ginger, and chilli; cook for about 5 minutes, stirring throughout.

3 Add squash and salt and cook until squash is tender.

4 Toss in the leafy greens, soy sauce, lemon juice, salt & pepper and cook for 1 minute.

CHEF'S NOTE
Ginger contains powerful anti-inflammatory and antioxidant properties.

A VEGGIE EXTRAVAGANZA!

Vegan Dinner

Ingredients

- 1 tbsp nut butter
- 150g/5oz firm tofu, cubed
- 250g/9oz celery, diced
- 500g/18oz baby spinach
- 250g/9oz cauliflower florets
- 500g/18oz shredded cabbage

- 250g/9oz green beans, chopped
- 500g/18oz diced courgette
- 1 onion, diced
- 250g/9oz diced turnip
- 1 green chilli, seeded and finely chopped

- 3 cloves garlic, finely grated
- Salt to taste
- Freshly ground pepper to taste
- 1½ lt/6 cups low sodium vegetable stock

Method

1 Sauté the garlic, onions & celery in nut butter for a few minutes over a medium heat.

2 Combine all the ingredients in a large saucepan or soup pot except for the baby spinach and place over medium to high heat.

3 Once it comes to a boil, reduce the heat to low and simmer for about 20 minutes, covered.

4 Adjust the seasonings if desired then stir in the baby spinach and cook or 30 seconds until wilted.

5 Serve into soup bowls.

CHEF'S NOTE
Process the soup with a bender if you prefer a smoother consistency.

HEALTHY VEGETABLE SAUTÉ

Vegan Dinner

Ingredients

- 2 tbsp extra virgin olive oil
- 1 tbsp minced garlic
- 1 large shallot, sliced
- 250g/9oz mushrooms, sliced
- 250g/9oz broccoli florets
- 250g/9oz artichoke hearts
- 250g/9oz baby peas

- 1 bunch asparagus, sliced into 3-inch pieces
- 250g/9oz cherry tomatoes, halved
- 1/2 tsp sea salt

For The Vinaigrette
- 3 tbsp white wine vinegar
- 6 tbsp extra-virgin olive oil
- 1/2 tsp sea salt
- 1 tsp ground oregano
- handful fresh parsley, chopped

Method

1 Add the oil to a frying pan set over medium heat. Stir in garlic and shallots and sauté for about 2 minutes.

2 Stir in mushrooms for about 5 minutes or until golden.

3 Stir in broccoli, artichokes, and asparagus and continue cooking for 5 more minutes.

4 Stir in peas, tomatoes and salt and cook for 2 more minutes.

5 Prepare vinaigrette by mixing together the vinegar, oil, salt, oregano and parsley in a bowl until well combined.

6 Serve vegetable sauté in a serving bowl and drizzle with vinaigrette.

7 Toss to combine and serve.

CHEF'S NOTE
Feel free to use whichever mix of vegetables you prefer in this simple sauté dish.

WHEAT BERRY AND BEAN CHILLI

Vegan
Dinner

Ingredients

- 500g/18oz cooked wheat berries
- 500g/18oz black beans, rinsed
- 250g/9oz chipotle peppers, minced
- 500g/18oz tinned chopped tomatoes
- 2 tbsp olive oil

- 1 yellow pepper, diced
- 1 yellow onion, diced
- 5 cloves garlic, minced
- 1 ½ tsp cumin powder
- 2 tsp red chilli powder
- 1 tsp dried oregano
- ½ tsp sea salt

- ½ tsp freshly ground black pepper
- 500ml/2 cups low sodium vegan stock
- 1 lime, juiced
- 125g/4oz freshly chopped coriander
- 1 avocado, cubed

Method

1 Place a casserole pot over a medium heat and add the olive oil.

2 Sauté the onions, garlic, yellow pepper, cumin, chilli powder, black pepper, oregano and salt until soft for about 5 minutes.

3 Add in the black beans, chipotle, tomatoes and stock, bring to a boil then lower the heat, cover and cook for half an hour.

4 Add the cooked wheat berries and cook for 5 more minutes until heated through.

5 Turn off the flame and add lime juice and garnish with coriander, lime and avocado cubes.

CHEF'S NOTE
Avocado, coriander & lime make a lovely fresh tasting topping to this dish.

FRESH AND YUMMY ZUCCHINI NOODLES

Vegan
Dinner

Ingredients

- For the Zucchini noodles:
- 4 Zucchini (courgettes)
- A pinch of sea salt
- Olive oil

For the Cashew cream:
- 250g/9oz raw cashews
- Clean drinking water
- 2 tbsp coconut milk
- Mild curry powder
- Freshly chopped mint to taste
- For serving:

- Yellow, sweet, tomatoes
- Baby salad greens
- Fresh chopped coriander
- Watermelon, mango or cantaloupe slices

Method

1 Start by peeling the courgettes and use a vegetable spiral slicer to make zucchini noodles.

2 Drizzle with olive oil and sprinkle with a small pinch of sea salt then toss well to combine and set aside.

3 Combine the cashew cream ingredients in a blender and pulse twice to form a crunchy sauce.

4 Arrange the baby salad greens followed by the tomatoes.

5 Serve the noodles at the center of the plate and finish off with the fruit pieces and garnish with coriander.

6 Serve immediately. Enjoy!

CHEF'S NOTE
Cashew nuts are a fantastic high fat vegan ingredient.

FRESH AND LIGHT VEGETABLE MEDLEY

Vegan Dinner

Ingredients

For the couscous:
- 160g/6oz pine nuts
- 2 heads cauliflower
- 2 tbsp extra virgin olive oil
- 1 tbsp raw agave
- 2 tbsp nutritional yeast
- Pepper & salt to taste

For the medley:
- 250g/9oz mushrooms
- 250g/9oz fresh corn
- 250g/9oz courgette, diced
- 250g/9oz fava beans, peeled
- 250g/9oz carrots, diced
- 2 tbsp extra virgin olive oil
- 2 tbsp freshly chopped basil
- 1 tbsp lemon juice

For the sauce:
- 60ml/¼ cup lemon juice
- 125g/4oz nama shoyu
- 3 tbsp raw agave
- 1 tbsp extra virgin olive oil

Method

1 Combine all the ingredients of the veggie medley in a large bowl and toss well to combine then set aside.

2 Next blend all the sauce ingredients in until well emulsified and smooth.

3 Now toss the couscous with the medley mixture in the large bowl.

4 Serve into individual serving bowls and drizzle with sauce and you are ready to eat.

CHEF'S NOTE
Try adding a handful of chopped parsley to the medley.

NUTTY KALE WRAPS

Vegan Dinner

Ingredients

- 4 really big kale leaves
- 250g/9oz pecans, raw
- 1 ripe avocado, sliced
- 80g/3oz alfalfa sprouts
- 1 red pepper, sliced

- ½ lemon
- 1 tsp extra virgin olive oil
- 1 tsp cumin
- ½ tsp grated ginger
- 1 tbsp tamari

Method

1 Cut off the stems from the kale and rinse them under running water to remove any grit. Soak them in warm water with the juice of half a lemon for about 10 minutes then dry the leaves using paper towels.

2 Shave of the central root so the leaves become easier to roll.

3 Add the nuts, cumin, and tamari, ginger and olive oil to your food processor and pulse until the mixture forms a ball-like shape.

4 Spread out the leaves and divide the pecan mix among the leaves. Top with sliced red pepper, avocado, alfalfa sprouts and drizzle lime juice on top.

5 Fold the top and bottom parts then roll up the sides. Slice the wrap in two, if desired and serve immediately. Enjoy!

CHEF'S NOTE
Don't worry if your wraps fall apart. They'll still taste great!

CUMIN SPICED MILLET PILAF 'ONE POT'

SERVES 4

Ingredients

- 500g/18oz organic millet
- 1 tbsp olive oil
- 1 tsp crushed cardamom
- 3 tsp cumin seeds
- 1 bay leaf

- 1 inch cinnamon stick
- 1 large white onion, chopped
- 1 tsp sea salt
- 750ml/3 cups vegan stock

Method

1 Set your instant pot to sauté mode and heat oil; sauté white onion, cardamom, cumin, bay leaf and cinnamon stick for about 1 minute.

2 Stir in onion and continue cooking for about 5 minutes.

3 Stir in millet, stock and salt.

4 Lock the lid and cook on high pressure for 1 minute.

5 When done, natural release pressure for about 10 minutes.

6 Fluff the millet with a fork and serve.

CHEF'S NOTE
If you don't have a one-pot you can use a slow cooker for this recipe.

VEGAN MEATLOAF

Vegan
Dinner

Ingredients

For The Meatloaf:
- 1 potato, shredded
- 250g/9oz quick oats
- 500g/18oz lentils, cooked
- 250g/9oz tomato sauce
- 1 onion, finely chopped
- 250g/9oz celery, finely chopped

- 1 tbsp ground flaxseed
- 1 tbsp minced garlic
- 2 tbsp warm water
- 1tbsp olive oil
- 1 tbsp fresh rosemary, chopped
- 1 tbsp fresh thyme, chopped
- 125g/4oz parsley, chopped

For The Glaze:
- ¼ tsp smoked paprika
- 2 tbsp vegan ketchup

Method

1 Preheat your oven to 350F/175C/Gas4.

2 Combine the water with the ground flaxseed in a mug and set aside.

3 Pour the olive oil in a skillet and place over medium heat.

4 Sauté the celery and onion and lightly season with salt and pepper of choice. Cook until tender then add in the garlic and cook until fragrant then turn off the heat.

5 Combine all the meat loaf ingredients including the flaxseed mixture, seasoning as desired. Mix well to ensure all ingredients are well combined.

6 Lightly grease a loaf pan and scoop the loaf mixture into the pan.

7 Combine the paprika and ketchup in a small bowl and brush it over the meatloaf.

8 Place the pan in the oven and bake for 50 minutes until well browned.

9 Remove from oven and let cool for 5-10 minutes before removing the loaf from the pan and slicing it up. Enjoy!

CHEF'S NOTE

Serve with lots of steamed greens drizzled with garlic oil.

ASIAN STEAMY POT

Ingredients

- 125g/4oz extra thin rice noodles
- 250g/9oz shiitake mushrooms, stemmed then thinly sliced
- 250g/9oz green beans, chopped
- 4 carrots, peeled and thinly sliced
- 4 green onions, thinly sliced

- 1 tbsp extra virgin olive oil
- 1½ lt/6 cups low sodium vegan veggie broth
- 2 tbsp fresh ginger root, grated
- 160ml/2/3 cup low sodium soy sauce
- 1 tsp hot pepper sauce

Method

1 Cook the rice noodles according to package instructions. Drain then cut into bite size lengths.

2 As the noodles are cooking, heat olive oil in a large saucepan over medium flame and sauté the mushrooms for 2 minutes until they start browning.

3 Stir in the broth, chilli sauce, soy sauce, and ginger then bring to a boil.

4 Add in all the veggies and simmer for 5 minutes until tender.

5 Serve the noodles on individual bowls then ladle over the veggie soup. Enjoy!

CHEF'S NOTE
This is a super simple dinner for weeknight evenings.

WHITE BEAN AND AVOCADO CLUB SANDWICH

Vegan Dinner

Ingredients

- 500g/18oz white cannellini beans, rinsed
- 125g/4oz sprouts (radish, alfalfa, broccoli)
- 1 seedless cucumber, thinly sliced
- 1 pearl onion, thinly sliced
- 2 tbsp extra virgin olive oil
- ¼ tsp freshly ground black pepper
- 12 slices multigrain vegan bread
- ½ tsp coarse sea salt
- 2 avocados, thinly sliced

Method

1 Combine the cannellini beans, pepper, oil and salt in a large mixing bowl and use the back of a fork to roughly mash the bean mixture then set aside.

2 Arrange 8 slices of bread on a clean surface and equally divide the bean mash among them. Top with the sliced onions, cucumber and sprouts. Lastly top with avocado and sprinkle with coarse sea salt.

3 Stack the sandwiches on top of each other to make 4 double sandwiches then top with the 4 remaining slices of bread.

4 Slice the sandwiches diagonally if desired. Enjoy!

CHEF'S NOTE
You don't have to have triple slices of bread if you prefer a traditional sandwich.

HEALTHY RAW PASTA

Vegan
Dinner

Ingredients

- 4 white mushrooms, sliced
- 4 black mushrooms, sliced
- 2 tomatoes
- 10 sundried tomatoes
- 2 cucumbers

- 1 shallot
- 10 dates
- 1 orange, juiced
- ¼ tsp curry powder
- ¼ tsp red chilli powder

Method

1 Combine all the ingredients apart from the mushrooms and cucumbers in your food processor and pulse until you get a thick paste.

2 You may add some water if you prefer a thinner sauce.

3 Pour the sauce over the sliced mushrooms and combine well until all the mushrooms are evenly coated.

4 Chill in the fridge for 30 minutes for all the flavours to meld.

5 When you are ready to serve, use a vegetable spiral slicer to spiralizer the cucumbers into noodles then serve into individual bowls.

6 Top with the mushrooms and drizzle with the sauce. Enjoy!

CHEF'S NOTE
Dates are a vegan superfood with their superb fibre and antioxidant qualities.

Snacks & Desserts

NO-COOK DATE & WALNUT FUDGE

Vegan Snacks & Desserts

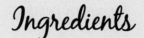

Ingredients

- 250g/9oz dried pitted dates
- 250g/9oz walnuts
- 1 tsp vanilla extract
- 4 tbsp cocoa powder

Method

1 In a food processor, combine all the ingredients and pulse until very smooth.

2 Spread the mixture in a pan and refrigerate until firm.

3 Cut into bars and enjoy!

CHEF'S NOTE
Try adding vegan chocolate chips if you wish.

ROASTED SPICED PUMPKIN SEEDS

Vegan Snacks & Desserts

Ingredients

- 250g/9oz shelled pumpkin seeds
- 2 tbsp fresh lime juice
- 1 tsp chilli powder
- Coarse salt

Method

1 Preheat the oven to 350°F/175C/Gas4.

2 Toss pumpkin seeds with fresh lime juice, chilli powder and sea salt until well coated.

3 Spread over a baking sheet and bake for about 20 minutes, stirring once.

4 Remove from oven and leave to cool before serving.

CHEF'S NOTE

Pumpkin seeds make a perfect power packed snack.

LIME RASPBERRY POPSICLES

Ingredients

- 1kg/36oz raspberries
- 1 tbsp lime juice
- 1 tsp lime zest

- 80ml/⅓ cup water
- ½ tsp liquid stevia

Method

1 Give the raspberries a rinse.

2 In a food processor combine all ingredients and pulse until very smooth.

3 Pour the mixture into Popsicle molds and freeze overnight.

4 Enjoy!

CHEF'S NOTE
Try serving with some vegan yoghurt to increase your fat intake.

SPICED CASHEW CREAM WITH FRUIT

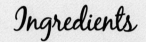

Vegan Snacks & Desserts

Ingredients

- 125g/4oz raw cashews, soaked for at least 30 minutes
- 1 tsp liquid stevia
- 125ml/½ cup hot water
- ½ tsp ground cinnamon
- Sea salt
- 1 Apple
- 1 pear

Method

1 De-stone, peel and thinly slice the apples & pear.

2 In a blender combine together the cashews, stevia, water and cinnamon.

3 Blend until very smooth.

4 Season and serve with the pear and apple slices.

CHEF'S NOTE
The cashew cream can be stored in the refrigerator for up to one week.

CHOCOLATE ORANGES

Vegan
Snacks &
Desserts

Ingredients

- 4 oranges, peeled and separated
- 200g/8oz vegan dark chocolate pieces
- 1 tbsp ground almonds
- Sea salt

Method

1 Line a baking tray with parchment paper.

2 Add the chocolate pieces to a small glass bowl and siting over a saucepan of boiling water on a medium to low heat.

3 Once the chocolate has melted stir in the almonds, take each orange slice and dip it halfway in the chocolate, place it onto the tray.

4 Place into the fridge to harden the chocolate.

5 Place them into a serving bowl and enjoy!

CHEF'S NOTE
This a is a lovely party 'nibble' to serve for guests with drinks.

COCONUT MILK FRUIT POPS

Vegan Snacks & Desserts

Ingredients

- 2 kiwis, peeled, halved & sliced
- 8 strawberries, halved & sliced
- 16 blueberries
- 16 raspberries
- 375ml/1½ cups coconut milk
- Popsicle molds

Method

1 Fill the Popsicle molds with an equal amount of the fruit.

2 Then fill with coconut milk to the top.

3 Place the Popsicle sticks on top of each, then place into the freezer and freeze for at least 5 hours or until solid.

4 Take them out of the freezer.

5 Enjoy!

CHEF'S NOTE
Keeping the fruit whole makes the popiscles look like the truly natural and healthy snack they are!

BERRY CRUMBLE

Ingredients

- 1kg/36oz fresh or frozen mixed berries
- 250g/9oz almond meal
- 125g/4oz almond butter

- 250g/9oz oven roasted walnuts, sunflower seeds, pistachios.
- ½ tsp ground cinnamon

Method

1 Preheat oven to 350°F/175C/Gas4.

2 Crush the nuts using a mortar and pestle.

3 In a bowl, use your thumbs and index fingers to combine together the nut mix, almond meal, cinnamon and almond butter to make crumbs.

4 In a pie dish, spread half the nut mixture over the bottom of the dish.

5 Top with the berries and finish with the rest of the nut mixture.

6 Bake for 30 minutes and serve warm.

CHEF'S NOTE
Try serving with natural vegan vanilla yoghurt.

MAPLE ROASTED PARSNIP CHIPS

Ingredients

- 1.25kg/45oz parsnips
- 60ml/¼ cup coconut oil
- 3 tbsp vegan maple syrup

Method

1 Preheat oven to 400F/200C/Gas6.

2 Peel the parsnips, cut them into chip sizes and place them into an oven proof dish.

3 Drizzle with coconut oil generously until covered and then do the same with the maple syrup.

4 Bake in the oven for 15 minutes and then turn them over.

5 Cook for a further 10-15 minutes or until they are crisp on the outside and tender inside.

6 Remove from oven and allow to cool before serving.

CHEF'S NOTE

The most important health benefits of parsnips include their ability to improve heart health.

BAKED APPLE CHIPS

Ingredients

- 3 apples
- ½ tsp ground cinnamon
- 1 tbsp brown sugar
- 2 tbsp chopped walnuts

Method

1 Preheat oven to 140F/275F/Gas1.

2 Line a baking tray with parchment paper and set aside.

3 Core the apples, slice thinly and place onto the baking tray.

4 Dust some cinnamon on top of them, sprinkle the sugar and place them into the oven for 40 minutes.

5 Flip the slices and cook for another 45mins-1hour or until the apples slices are dried up and crispy hour.

6 Take them out of the oven and allow them to cool and combine with the chopped walnuts.

CHEF'S NOTE
Cinnamon and sugar makes a classic combination.

NUTTY DATE ROLLS

Vegan
Snacks &
Desserts

Ingredients

- 250g/9oz cashew nuts
- 1 tbsp orange juice
- Desiccated coconut flakes
- 180g/6oz pitted dates

- 125g/4oz trail mix
- 1 tbsp almond meal
- 1 tbsp ground cinnamon

Method

1 Place the nuts, dates, trail mix, almond meal and cinnamon into the food processor.

2 Blend using a grinding blade (add in the orange juice when the blades stick).

3 Sprinkle the coconut over an area of the worktop.

4 Shape the mixture into rolls or balls, in the palm of your hand.

5 Roll the balls in the coconut.

6 Refrigerate in an airtight container.

CHEF'S NOTE

Dates are a good source of various vitamins and minerals including calcium, iron, phosphorus, potassium, magnesium and zinc.

SESAME CAULIFLOWER ROUNDS

Ingredients

- 1kg/36oz cauliflower flowerets, roughly chopped
- 3 tbsp coconut oil, melted
- 80g/3oz sesame seeds
- 2 tbsp chia seeds
- 60g/2oz golden flaxseed meal
- 1 tsp sea salt
- 80ml/⅓ cup water
- 250g/9oz toasted sesame seeds

Method

1 In a food processor whizz the cauliflower into 'rice' texture.

2 Add melted coconut oil, sesame seeds, chia seeds, flaxseed meal, salt and water and continue processing until dough is formed.

3 Chill for about 3 hours.

4 Preheat oven to 300F/150C/Gas2.

5 Line a large baking sheet with paper.

6 Scoop teaspoonful's of the dough and roll into balls.

7 Roll the balls into toasted sesame seeds and arrange them on the baking sheet.

8 Bake for about 30 minutes or until the balls are dry in the center.

CHEF'S NOTE
Let the rounds cool completely before serving.

CUCUMBER ROLLS

Vegan
Snacks &
Desserts

Ingredients

- 1 medium cucumber
- 2 tbsp sliced toasted almonds
- 2 tbsp finely diced black olives
- 2 tbsp diced roasted red pepper
- 1 clove roasted garlic, mashed
- ¼ cup coconut yoghurt

- A pinch of saffron
- 1 tbsp minced parsley
- ¼ tsp salt
- Pepper
- Chive stems for tying the rolls

Method

1 Slice the cucumber lengthwise into long and thin strips

2 Arrange the strips onto paper towel to absorb excess moisture.

3 In a large bowl, stir together almonds, black olives, red pepper, garlic, yoghurt, saffron, parsley, salt and pepper until well combined.

4 Make rolls by placing heaped teaspoonful's of the almond mixture on one end on a cucumber strip and rolling to enclose the filling.

5 Tie with chive stems and repeat with the remaining ingredients.

6 Chill before serving.

CHEF'S NOTE
Olives are very high in vitamin E and other powerful antioxidants.

COCONUT OIL ROASTED BEETROOT

Vegan Snacks & Desserts

Ingredients

- 2½lb/1.1kg beets, peeled and diced
- 4 tbsp coconut oil, melted
- ½ tsp coarse salt

Method

1 Preheat oven to 400F/200C/Gas6.

2 Spread the beets on a rimmed baking sheet and drizzle with coconut oil.

3 Sprinkle with sea salt and toss until well coated.

4 Bake for about 1 hour or until the beets are crispy and slightly caramelized.

CHEF'S NOTE
Beetroot is not only a good addition to your diet, it also protects your heart, bones & body.

BERRYLICIOUS ANTIOXIDANT-RICH POPS

Vegan Snacks & Desserts

Ingredients

- 375ml/1 ½ cups coconut milk or yoghurt
- 375g/13oz fresh blueberries
- 375g/13oz fresh blackberries
- 2 tbsp fresh lemon juice
- 1 tsp liquid stevia

Method

1 In a blender, blend together all the ingredients until very smooth.

2 Pour the mixture into molds and add the stick.

3 Freeze for about 6 hours.

CHEF'S NOTE

You can store these in the freezer for up to 2 months.

ROASTED CHILLI-VINEGAR PEANUTS

Ingredients

- 1 tbsp coconut oil
- 500g/18oz raw peanuts, unsalted
- 2 tsp sea salt

- 2 tbsp apple cider vinegar
- 1 tsp chilli powder
- 1 tsp fresh lime zest

Method

1 Preheat oven to 350F/175C/Gas4.

2 In a large bowl, toss together the coconut oil, peanuts, and salt until well coated.

3 Transfer to a rimmed baking sheet and roast in the oven for about 15 minutes or until fragrant.

4 Transfer the roasted peanuts to a bowl and add vinegar, chilli powder and lime zest.

5 Toss to coat well and serve.

CHEF'S NOTE
At least half of the fat in peanuts is heart-healthy monounsaturated fat.

TAHINI HUMMUS

Vegan
Snacks &
Desserts

Ingredients

- 2 tbsp extra-virgin olive oil
- 60g/2oz toasted sesame tahini
- 60g/2oz apple cider vinegar
- 250g/9oz tinned chickpeas

- 1 clove garlic, minced
- ½ tsp ground cumin
- 1 tsp sea salt
- 3 tbsp water

Method

1 Drain and rinse the chickpeas. Dry off with a paper towel.

2 Call ingredients in a food processor and blend.

3 Pulse until very smooth adding a little more oil if needed to loosen it up.

CHEF'S NOTE
Serve with carrots or cucumber slices.

HEALTHY SEED CRACKERS

Vegan
Snacks &
Desserts

Ingredients

- 1 tsp sea salt
- 125g/4oz raw buckwheat
- 125g/4oz linseeds

- 375g/13oz sunflower seeds
- 60g/2oz chia seeds
- 375ml/1½ cups warm water

Method

1 Mix together all ingredients in a large bowl.

2 Set aside for about 20 minutes, stirring occasionally.

3 Preheat oven to 325F/165C/Gas3.

4 Press the mixture into a baking tray lined with baking paper.

5 Bake for about an hour or until golden and crisp.

6 Remove from oven and cut into pieces.

CHEF'S NOTE

One ounce of sunflower seeds contains nearly 50 percent of the recommended daily value of vitamin E - which is an important fat-soluble vitamin.

Bonus Vegan
Drinks

We've also included a bonus section of drinks to enjoy on your vegan diet. These aren't necessarily all high in fat but will provide a great complementary addition to your diet.

If you wish to increase the fat intake in any of the blended smoothie or juice recipes; nuts, oil, nut butter, seeds, avocado, almond milk, coconut milk & vegan yoghurt all make good additions.

DELICIOUS STRAWBERRY PUNCH

Vegan Drinks

Ingredients

- 250g/9oz fresh strawberries
- 1lt/4 cups diet ginger ale
- 1 litre/4 cups fresh pineapple juice

Method

1 Remove the green tops off the strawberries.

2 Place in a blender and process the strawberries until smooth.

3 Add ginger ale and pineapple juice and chill to serve.

CHEF'S NOTE
Garnish with lime or lemon wedges, if desired.

CITRUS PUNCH

Vegan
Drinks

Ingredients

- 250g/9oz fresh chopped pineapple
- 125ml/½ cup freshly squeezed lemon juice
- 750ml/3 cups water
- 250ml/1 cup lemonade, frozen

Method

1 In a food processor, puree fresh pineapple.

2 Combine the pureed pineapple with the remaining ingredients.

3 Chill for at least 1 hour to serve.

CHEF'S NOTE
Try mango instead of pineapple if you like.

GINGERY LEMONADE

SERVES 4

Vegan
Drinks

Ingredients

- 14 slices fresh ginger root
- 1.5 litres/6 cups water
- 1 tsp stevia

- 250ml/1cup fresh lemon juice
- 1 lemon, sliced

Method

1 Combine ginger root, water and stevia in a saucepan set over medium heat.

2 Bring to a gentle boil.

3 Remove from heat and stir in lemon juice.

4 Let cool for about 15 minutes and chill for at least 1 hour.

5 Serve over ice garnished with lemon slices.

CHEF'S NOTE
Fresh lemonade on a hot day is unbeatable.

LIME LEMON SLUSH

Vegan
Drinks

Ingredients

- 2 limes
- 2 lemons
- 1 tbsp liquid stevia

- 250ml/1 cup pure water
- Ice

Method

1 Peel & de-seed the lemon and lime (unless you have a Nutribullet or similar super-powerful blender).

2 Add all the ingredients to the blender add process until smooth.

3 Serve

CHEF'S NOTE

This a super zingy drink. Adjust the balance of citrus and stevia to get the taste just right for you.

GINGERY GRAPE JUICE

Vegan
Drinks

Ingredients

- 500g/18oz red grapes
- 2-inch piece fresh ginger

- 1 medium lemon, peeled, juiced
- 125ml/½ cup water

Method

1 Destalk all the grapes (make sure they are seedless) and peel the fresh ginger root.

2 Combine all ingredients in a blender.

3 Blend until very smooth.

4 Enjoy!

CHEF'S NOTE
Grapes contain antioxidants that help fight free radicals in the body.

FAT-BURNER JUICE

Vegan
Drinks

Ingredients

- 250g/9oz greens leaves
- 2 celery stalks
- 2 green apples
- 2 carrots

- 1 red pepper
- 1 lemon
- 1 ginger

Method

1 Peel & core the apple.

2 De-seed the red pepper.

3 Peel and de-seed the lemon (unless you have a nutribullet or similar super-powerful blender).

4 Juice everything together.

5 Enjoy!

CHEF'S NOTE
The vitamin C in peppers helps aid the proper absorption of iron.

GARLICKY GREEN JUICE

Vegan Drinks

Ingredients

- 1 green apple
- 250g/9oz kale
- 1 celery stalk
- 1 clove garlic
- Ginger
- Ice

Method

1 Peel & core the apple.

2 Peel the garlic clove.

3 Peel and de-seed the lemon (unless you have a Nutribullet or similar super-powerful blender).

4 Peel the fresh ginger root.

5 Juice everything together and enjoy!

CHEF'S NOTE

Consuming garlic on a daily basis helps to lower cholesterol levels because of the anti-oxidant properties of Allicin.

THE SUPER-8 DETOX JUICE

Vegan
Drinks

Ingredients

- 50g/2oz spinach
- 4 kale leaves
- 1 broccoli floret
- 1 tomato

- ½ red pepper
- 1 carrot
- 1 stalk of celery
- Handful of parsley

Method

1 De-seed the red pepper.

2 Cut any thick stalks off the kale.

3 Juice everything together and top up the glasses with crushed ice or water.

4 Enjoy!

CHEF'S NOTE

Detox drinks can reduce inflammation, boost energy and speed up weight gain.

KALE-BEETROOT JUICE

Vegan
Drinks

Ingredients

- 2 leaves of Kale
- 1 apple, cored
- 2 carrots, chopped
- 1 stalk of celery, chopped
- 1 small beetroot, chopped

Method

1 Peel & core the apple.

2 Blend everything together and top up the glass
with crushed ice or water.

3 Enjoy!

CHEF'S NOTE
Beetroot is of exceptional nutritional value;
especially the greens, which are rich in
calcium, iron and vitamins A and C.

GINGERY PINEAPPLE PARADISE

Vegan Drinks

Ingredients

- 1-inch piece fresh ginger
- 125g/4oz pineapple chunks
- 2 tbsp lime juice

- 1 apple
- 125g/4oz mango chunks

Method

1 Peel & core the apple.

2 Peel the fresh ginger root.

3 Juice everything together.

4 Serve over ice and enjoy.

CHEF'S NOTE

Light and fresh, try this fruity drink in the morning with some chopped nuts on top.

IMMUNE BOOSTER SHOT

Vegan
Drinks

Ingredients

- 1 knob of ginger
- 250ml/1 cup water
- 2 tbsp apple cider vinegar
- ½ tsp cayenne pepper

- 1 tsp turmeric
- ½ tsp pepper
- 1 tsp liquid stevia
- ice

Method

1 Peel the fresh ginger root.

2 Juice everything together and serve.

CHEF'S NOTE
Cayenne pepper is always a potent addition to any food. Adjust the quantity to suit your own taste.

BLOODY HOT THIN MARY

*Vegan
Drinks*

Ingredients

- 250ml/1 cup fresh tomato juice
- 4 tbsp apple cider vinegar
- Pinch of cayenne pepper
- 3 dashes Worcestershire sauce

- 1 tsp hot sauce
- Freshly ground black pepper
- Pinch of celery salt

Method

1 Stir together all ingredients.

2 Serve over ice.

CHEF'S NOTE

The antioxidant qualities of tomatoes are particularly good for fresh healthy skin.

MINT CHOCOLATE COFFEE SMOOTHIE

Vegan Drinks

Ingredients

- 180ml/ ¾ cup brewed coffee, chilled
- 1 tbsp coconut milk
- ¼ tsp cocoa powder

- 3 drops dark chocolate stevia
- 3 drops peppermint stevia
- Ice cubes

Method

1 Blend all ingredients until very smooth.

2 Serve garnished with mint.

CHEF'S NOTE

Adjust the chocolate and peppermint stevia quantities to suit your own taste

DETOXIFYING TURMERIC TEA

Vegan Drinks

Ingredients

- 375ml/1 ½ cups boiling water
- 1 bag of chamomile tea
- 1 bag of peppermint tea
- 1 tbsp coconut milk
- ½ tsp vanilla extract

- 1 tsp turmeric
- 1 tsp ginger
- 1/4 tsp pepper
- 1 tsp liquid stevia

Method

1 In a large mug, combine hot water, chamomile and peppermint teas.

2 Leave to steep for at least 3 minutes.

3 Stir in the remaining ingredients.

4 Serve hot!

CHEF'S NOTE
The root of turmeric has been used in traditional medicine around the world for hundreds of years.

MATCHA MILK SHAKE

Vegan
Drinks

Ingredients

- 250ml/1 cup unsweetened almond milk
- ½ tsp matcha powder

Method

1 Heat the almond milk in a pan until almost boiled.

2 Add matcha powder in a serving mug and pour in hot almond milk.

3 Whisk until well blended.

CHEF'S NOTE
Matcha is high in a catechin called EGCG which is believed to have cancer-fighting effects on the body.

YOU MAY ALSO ENJOY....

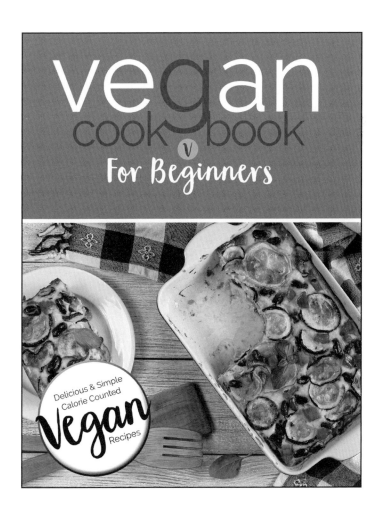

Delicious & Simple Calorie Counted Vegan Recipes